# The Vista Sisters

## Jams, Jellies, and Jesus

Virginnia Swenson and

Marjorie Gores

ISBN 978-1-64492-435-8 (paperback)
ISBN 978-1-64492-436-5 (digital)

Christian Faith Publishing, Inc.
832 Park Avenue
Meadville, PA 16335
www.christianfaithpublishing.com

Printed in the United States of America

Here comes the
# Jam Van!

It was very early one morning when a customer who had received a sampler of jams and jellies called me and said,

> "Hey, Charlie. You know those Vista Sisters? Tell me, are they for real?"

> "You bet they're real! So, what jam are you eating?"

> "Boysenberry."

—Charlie M

# Contents

# Vista: Idyllic and Ideal

*The Covenant Companion*

Once upon a time...

# The Vista Sisters:

## Virginnia Swenson and Marjorie Gores

**About Us**

We were born in the Great Depression years 1929 and 1933, on a farm in Southern Minnesota. Sometimes referred to as the dirty thirties, it was a time before electricity, indoor plumbing, and the madness leading to WWII. Life was simple but hard work. Egg money was to buy groceries, and cows were our source of milk and contentment.

Vista is the name chosen by Swedish immigrants who first settled this territory around the 1850s. Located in South Central Minnesota between New Richland and Waseca, it is made up of farms surrounding the focal point of two churches.

The usual creamery, bank, and grocery store were three miles away in a small village named Otisco.

As Dad had the harder daily outdoor work, Mom was usually at his side. I would milk 1–2 cows, Marge 2–4, and Mom would milk the remainder.

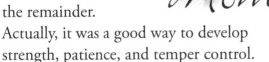

Actually, it was a good way to develop strength, patience, and temper control. To milk cows requires a gentle touch. Getting the last of the milk (called stripping) is the same technique I use to strip the elderberries from the stems. Honest!

7

Gathering eggs, especially from cluck hens, was a challenge but worth it. The eggs were wonderful in flavor and color. Mom made the best cakes, breads, and breakfast with homemade sausage. In our day, everything was grass fed and healthy.

## Always a Garden

Because of the depression and WWII, we had a large garden. There was food rationing, and it was not uncommon for our parents to share our produce with our city relatives. We knew we were blessed to be stewards of the land.

Because there were no freezers yet, Mom did a lot of canning. She tried to preserve as much as possible from fruit, vegetables, and even meat. In the summer, it was too hot to fire up the cook stove, so Mom would use the two-burner kerosene stove. This is when I first remember her making jams and jellies. Our cookware was lightweight and heated up quickly. One had to watch for the right phase to add the pectin and the sugar. It could be a nerve-wracking experience, but it taught us patience under fire, so to speak. Instead of lids, melted paraffin was poured on top of filled jars to seal them.

We had our own strawberry patch, raspberries, grapes,

plums, rhubarb, and apples. Nothing was better in the winter than a dish of our canned sauce and crackers before bedtime.

Flowers were a big part of gardening, if only for their beauty. Mom had rows of flowers of many varieties. People would come by just to look (early garden walks) or even ask for some flowers for a wedding or party. Mom always said yes.

## Times Change

We started to miss our togetherness when Marge started high school and I was still in country school. She is four years older, so when she graduated high school, I started. The same happened with college. Even our summers changed. I stayed home and worked while Marge worked each summer at various jobs.

In 1955, our lives really changed as Marge married Jim, a tall Texan. That June day, our country church was decorated with local flowers, and joy overflowed as vows were exchanged.

This church was the base of our entire upbringing and the center of our activities. It was a church our grandparents

helped build. After the honeymoon, they left to start their life together in California. Two weeks later, I left for Cheyenne, Wyoming, and airline training as a flight attendant for United Airlines. As far as I can remember, this was my dream.

## Life Goes On

Mom and Dad adjusted to being empty nesters. After twenty very happy years, Jim passed away. Two years later, our dad also went home to be with the Lord. This left Mom alone on the farm, Marge alone, and I was alone. Marge moved home from California, and when I retired, I also moved back to the farm. It seemed the natural thing to do.

## Common Sense and Education

Our parents never went to high school, but they learned how to apply their knowledge to life. Marge and I walked a mile each day to country school. In winter, we climbed formidable snowdrifts. In spring and fall, we avoided

puddles or sloughs if we cut across
the fields. We listened to
meadowlarks and dodged
snakes. Each time we
came home, there was
that wonderful aroma
of freshly baked cookies,
fried doughnuts, or fresh
bread. We usually saw
Mom looking for us out
the kitchen window. She
knew, and we knew, we were
safe.

## In Times of War

As early as eight years old, I was out hoeing in the bean fields
along with Marge and lots of other kids. The men were off to
war; canning companies needed help, and migrant workers
were unavailable. As years went on, machinery did the
cultivation, but we had learned to appreciate the land.
We were taught the Earth is the Lord's. Marge was older; she

helped turn cut hemp for
drying before it was made
into rope. She also got special
clearance to work on radios
for the war effort. We were
all proud and excited to help
the cause. After all, there were
posters everywhere of Uncle
Sam looking at us and saying,
"I need YOU."

County News/Char Ranking

## Our Purpose—Two-Fold

While our jams and jellies were strictly after recipes in common use, it seemed the public was impressed with our product. If we missed a Saturday market, we heard that people were asking, "Where are the jam ladies? You know, the gals from Otisco." or "Those two sisters," and so on. Worried what else we might be called, we came up with the logical one: the Vista Sisters!

As we became acquainted with our community and Waseca County, we found ourselves more and more interested in missions.

"We're doing this for the Lord because we find great joy in it and because we're mission-minded," says Marjorie. "I can't believe people buying stuff for themselves all the time, and not looking around and seeing the needs of people near and far. It gives us pleasure that we are being given the strength and the ability."

Thanks to the Vista Sisters' dedication, a new generation can watch and learn how to give purposefully, sacrificially, and joyfully.

—December 2010,
*The Covenant Companion*

We were raised to support the mission work around the world so that was a given for us. At first, the proceeds went toward our personal mission causes. But, after our second trip to India, and seeing the famine, we decided to give all our market proceeds toward their famine relief. To our amazement, our sales doubled and we knew the Lord was giving His blessing on us. We are truly blessed!

What a beautiful time of the year to be alive. I am enjoying my coffee and watching the early birds as the sun comes up. We even have a visible pair of cardinals. The farm work still goes on, although the rototiller seems a little heavier this year.

We have eleven acres to tend (but the fields are rented out). Some are for flowers and some are for vegetable gardens. So far I have nineteen varieties of jams/jellies for the farmers market.

(Virginia Swenson, New Richland RUACA, 2006)

Even though we get tired, we know why and for whom we are working. The Lord lightens our load and we have a good time. As Mom would say, "If you can't work, where's the fun?" We look at each other (when we're tired) and ask, "Are we having fun yet?" We usually laugh and get back to our task. Without the Lord's blessing and presence, we would have to quit. *It's a partnership!*

In retirement, two sisters were looking for a way to connect to their community. They discovered a way to make a difference in the world.
—Marianne Peters,
*The Covenant Companion*

# Organizations

## Bibles for the World

"You must come and hear this
speaker. This man and
his mission will change
your lives" This was
our introduction to
Bibles for the World,
and we did go hear Dr.
Ro Pudaite speak at the
Missionary Fellowship
meeting in Austin, MN.
Their goal was to fill the

chuckholes that hamper the work of the
missionary in the field by providing a typewriter, bike, or
whatever item they needed to ease their work. (Their story is
in a book, *The Million-Dollar Living Room* by Krause.)

As usual, we were running late and Dr. Pudaite was already
speaking. I must say we were smitten immediately by his
message. Tie's not a tall man, but a giant in love, joy, and zeal
for the Lord. Over coffee, we learned of all the projects that
BFW is engaged in: Bible distribution all over the world,
schools for the Hmar tribe (primarily in Manipur), building
a well-equipped modem hospital, maintaining a seminary,
and providing education for grades 1–12 through child
sponsorship (Marge and I are sponsoring nine children).

In 2003, we made our first trip to northeast India to the
city of Sielmat, Manipur, which is the home of the Pudaite
family. That year, we all celebrated the first graduation and
dedication of sixteen pastors and had the joy of presenting
their Bibles. We also became honorary members of the Hmar

tribe, with all the privileges and *opportunities* (key word) bestowed upon us.

Our second trip to India was in 2006, just as the fifty-year famine affecting northeast India was at its peak. This is the year we decided to give all the market proceeds toward famine relief, and we also saw our attention turn to the "modern" city of Chandigarh. The idea of winning Chandigarh to the Lord section by section was a spirit-led decision for Dr. Pudaite. Our decision to support the startup of this mission field led to times of challenges. We made a side trip to Chandigarh and met Thanga, the area missionary and also the home church family. It was a lovely time of fellowship.

In 2008, we made our third trip to India to revive our friendship with the Hmar people and visit with our sponsored children. We also saw the fantastic expansion of the hospital, school system, and seminary. The Lord is truly a blessing!

Between the two of us, we have nine sponsored children who are receiving a wonderful faith-filled education, and they will excel in life as they grow. What a thrill it was to receive letters telling me they have become born-again.

We also returned to Chandigarh to see the growth of the church communities. It now goes beyond the city as the Christian workers spread the good news to their home areas. The Lord laid the burden of Chandigarh on the heart of Thanga, and the Holy Spirit is accomplishing marvelous things through Thanga's teaching of scriptures and his leadership training.

## Chandigarh—how important is it?

When Dr. Pudaite presented the idea of winning Chandigarh sector by sector, my sister and I were caught up in the vision. We made the payment for our sector (#39) in April of 2006. My comment at the time was "The devil isn't going to like this," and that turned out to be an understatement.

The devil caused many malfunctions: (1) Our dishwasher needed repair, (2) The shed air conditioner needed to be totally repaired, (3) A sensor in my van went out, (4) A lightning bolt knocked out our air exchanger panel, (5) Our home air conditioner needed replacement, (6) October 22, 2006, we arrived home in Minnesota from India to a very cold house. Our boiler had exploded, causing layers of soot in our basement and throughout the entire house, so we needed a new furnace.

God's blessings are wonderful: (1) Our house didn't burn down, (2) ServiceMaster came and took care of the cleaning, (3) most all was covered by insurance, and (4) the great beauty is Chandigarh is alive and growing rapidly. So *shout to the Lord* for Chandigarh and win it sector by sector. If the devil is so worried about Chandigarh that he caused all these mishaps to happen to two sisters in Minnesota, you can believe Chandigarh is extremely important. (VS)

We had a suite in Imphal! Only place for mosquito protection.

Kaziranga National Park

Taj Mahal, India, 2003

## *Chandigarh*

*My name is Amethyst from Chandigarh*

*Train a child in the way he should go and when he is old he will not turn from it*

# Bibles for the World Reaches India's Far Northwest Corner

By Dr. Rochunga Pudaite

   With the many rapid changes occurring in India, we're very grateful that God has opened a new door in the Northwest—a door that we plan to enter in 2006. Two years ago, one of our national missionaries was sent out to Chandigarh, a city that has a reputation for being very resistant to the Gospel.

   I'd like to tell you a little about this interesting city, and of the strategic plan God has given us to reach it.

Dr. Rochunga Pudaite

   When India gained independence in 1947, the Northwestern state of Punjab was split in two. The state's original capital, Lahore, in the western half, became a part of Pakistan. This left the Indian side of Punjab without a capital. Soon the government approved a site for a new one. With

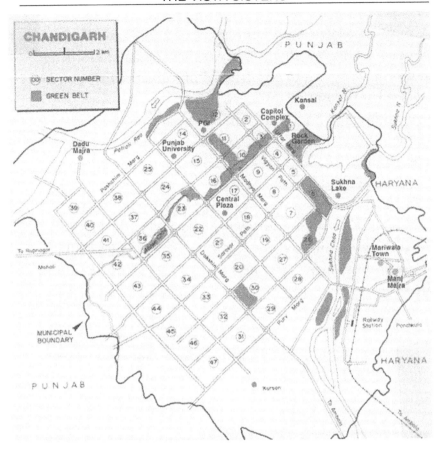

Chandigarh, a city divided into 47 sectors

the help of a French architect, the city was designed, and named Chandigarh (which in English means "the home of the goddess Chandi"). It became the capital of two bordering states, Punjab and Haryan.

Unique to Chandigarh is its sense of order. In the past, many Indian cities were built randomly and chaotically. Chandigarh is a happy exception to this rule. It is well-planned, carefully laid out in numbered sectors, as the map here shows.

When Mawii and I went in October 2005, we were amazed at how orderly the city was, how organized its design. It was our first visit to our national missionaries there, and we rejoiced at the amazing works of God.

Although Chandigarh has long been considered very difficult to evangelize, our missionaries have been seeing a great hunger for God. Their churches are rapidly growing, with many Hindus, Kihns, and Muslims coming to know Christ.

And as always in India, when asked what the biggest needs were, our missionaries replied, "This city needs Bibles. Most of these people have never seen a Bible in their entire lives."

Home church in Petella, India—a branch of the mission in Chandigarh

## Sielmat

Dr. Ro, as a young child, was sent through the jungle to begin his education in a remote school.

His father, the chief of the Hmar tribe, told young Ro the school was located "beyond the next mountain." This expression became the title for his book and CD.

We were privileged to visit the school area as depicted in the picture.

## Bible Quizzing a New Hit in Northeast India

Finalists in the 2005 Bible Quizzing tournament, held at the Bibles for the World school in Sielmat, Manipur

New believers in Chandigarh working toward their goal: to distribute 500,000 copies of John's Gospel to their Sikh and Hindu neighbors

## Headhunters to Hearthunters

The Hmar Children

The people of the Hmar (mar) tribe of northeast India were fierce headhunters. In 1910, a missionary, Watkin Roberts, sent the Gospel of John to a Hmar chief. The chief invited Roberts to come and explain the Scriptures. He went, despite a travel ban by the British Colonial riders, and five young tribesmen chose to follow the Lord Jesus. The converts grew in faith and became leaders of a new and growing church. Within two generations, the entire tribe was evangelized. Head hunting stopped and "hearthunting" began. They now carry the Gospel to their neighboring tribes and the regions beyond.

Article from the Quarterly Newsletter for Friends and Partners of Bibles for the World, June 2003, Vol. 32, No. 2

SAVIO ENGLISH SCHOOL
A project of Patnership Mission Society

Sielmat—the Pudaites' home area

Families waiting outside Sielmat Hospital, 2003

Synagogue in Sielmat

Hospital entrance, dedication March 2014

Virginnia, Mawii, Dr. Ro, Marjorie

James, Marge, Calvin (sponsored children)

Dorothy and Virginnia, first sponsored

## The Caste System

India is so diverse from one state to another. Each state can have several languages or dialects. One Indian pastor told us he felt like a stranger traveling in his own country. BFW prints Bibles in various languages and in English, which many people speak.

The caste system is such an unjust system. The Dalits are the lowest caste but perhaps more open to Christianity. The Dalits live a simple, hard life and aren't blinded by materialism and the world as a whole. I equate it to the shepherds being the first to hear the good news of the birth of the Christ. The shepherds were the lowest caste and believed without a doubt and worshipped Christ. This leads to the unique ministry that BFW has with the Dalits.

The Hmar tribe is not really in the caste system, as all of northeastern India is made up of other unknown tribes. (VS)

First school in all Hindu area at Chingrawali

by Rochunga Pudaite

Joining us on our recent trip were a number of our friends from the United States, most of whom were visiting India for the first time. Here are just a few highlights of our time together visiting my homeland and a number of places in which Bibles for the World is having an impact for God's Kingdom...

Christian Education in India Is a Growing Force for Christ...

We visited three schools in Delhi run by Pastor Raj and Pastor Azad, truly wonderful men. They both have schools and churches that they have started and that they now lead. We visited two crowded classrooms and one outside presentation in a Dalit slum. Pastor Raj told us about the Christian club he has formed for students and parents, growth in his church, conversions of students and their families, and recent baptisms of new believers. Both pastors have many Hindu parents of schoolchildren who have begun attending their churches.

The Partnership Parents Program through the Partnership Mission Society (PMS) provides an opportunity for a Christian education for kids who would not otherwise have this chance.

*Delhi*

Outside a new home church in Delhi—with Thanga

Singing praises in mission churches at Delhi

Primitive church survived demolition because it was a church. It had one door, no windows, chairs only for the guests, no standing room at all, but everyone was happy.

Bible study with Mawii Pudaite

# *Chingrawali*

For Marjorie Gores and Virginia Swenson

January 2008

Subject: Report from James S. Sanate, Chingrawali

Beloved friends and Prayer Supporters,

Wishing you a happy New Year!

On Nov. 04, 2007, God gave us a lovely baby boy, and we named him Benjamin Lalthanglawr. It is so wonderful to become a father. At this moment they (Margaret and Benjamin) are back at home with my parents in Shillong. God willing, they will be joining us by the middle of March '08. Thank you for your prayers for us. As you can imagine, I am looking forward to our reunion!

We are always happy knowing that you are always standing by us in time of our needs. Carrying out the Lord's ministry would have been much more difficult without your prayer support and help. Knowing that you are always with us gives us strength, encouragement, and joy.

As we begin this New Year, we ask you to keep us constantly in your prayer, so that we may not lose strength to carry on.

It has been a year and a half since we started a school ministry, mainly focusing on the Dalits. Though we are focusing on the Dalits, there is a danger in exposing our vision and mission for the Dalits. We are cautious that the high castes might feel that we are raising an army against them. We need to be "as wise as a serpent, but harmless as a dove."

As they gain more knowledge in school, the students are starting to dream for their future. This is encouraging to watch. There are a few students who are even doing much better than the upper castes. We hope that God will make the school as the model for the transformation of the nation. Even though the Dalits (untouchable outcasts) may become educated there is still a strong feeling that they are to serve the upper caste. We are trying and working hard to help change this mindset

You will be surprised to know that, although the Dalits are also Hindus by religion, most of the Dalits have never visited Hindu temples, nor keep a Hindu god or goddess in their homes. They are not allowed to step in the temples as they are "untouchables." They are so oppressed by the upper-caste Hindus. They are eager to hear the love of God and about heaven. Most of them are without religion. We need to pray that the Holy Spirit may work within them. If the Holy Spirit is not working along with us, it is impossible to explain the work and love of Christ. What we need most at the hour is the mighty work of the Holy Spirit.

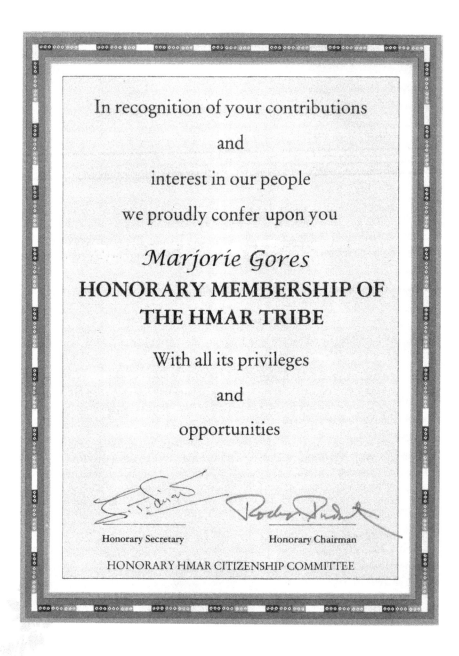

In recognition of your contributions

and

interest in our people

we proudly confer upon you

*Marjorie Gores*

## HONORARY MEMBERSHIP OF THE HMAR TRIBE

With all its privileges

and

opportunities

Honorary Secretary          Honorary Chairman

HONORARY HMAR CITIZENSHIP COMMITTEE

*Virginia Swenson*

In recognition of your contributions

and

interest in our people

we proudly confer upon you

an

# HONORARY MEMBERSHIP OF THE HMAR TRIBE

With all its privileges

and

opportunities

Honorary Secretary             Honorary Chairman

HONORARY HMAR CITIZENSHIP COMMITTEE

## Mission Aviation Fellowship

It all began after we each received a form letter from MAF emphasizing how important it was for them to have exposure to the public and asking us to become advocates. Many letters had come requesting funds for a newly developed plane—the Kodiak 100.

The Kodiak 100 has a larger carrying capacity and uses jet fuel instead of AV gas. It uses an extremely short runway for takeoff and landing, making it ideal for use in rugged remote areas. Therefore, the request at our age, no computer or e-mail, seemed impossible to Virginnia, who threw her request away; I filed mine away under "later." Two days later, I brought MAF's letter to her attention again. She leaned back in her chair, sighed, and said, "Well, the only thing I can think of to help is to have a fly-in!"

"Oh my," I said. "That's a big deal. I need a sign before we tackle that." We prayed.

Two days later on Sunday at church, where we were newcomers attending for the second time, we heard a specific prayer for MAF. We poked each other and agreed immediately that this was our sign. Virginnia spoke to the member who had prayed. He smiled and said, "God works in mysterious ways." We discovered the airport manager was not only a church member, but was also actively engaged in annual visits overseas to service MAF aircraft. He had two possible Saturdays to schedule a visit from MAF.

When our MAF contact in Nampa, Idaho, realized where Waseca, Minnesota, was, she said, "Why, that's right along our route to Oshkosh, Wisconsin, where our plane is being featured all week at the air show."

The new Kodiak 100 landed in Waseca, Minnesota, and the rest is history. The Lord's hand was evident everywhere. A couple from church walked up to us at the next farmers market to become acquainted as their son was a manager of a MAF station overseas. They and others from the church took over many responsibilities and lifted that load from us. The fly-in was a great success with 250–300 people attending. Everyone had a hands-on experience with the Kodiak 100. MAF president John Boyd said it was an experience that needed to be repeated across the country to introduce MAF and its program to the public. Believe me! The Vista Sisters were ecstatic and exhausted, but we still praise the Lord for opening this window of opportunity to support MAF through our farmers market sales. (MG)

Open house at Waseca Airport

Church helpers

MAF team reflecting and relaxing after fly-in

# KICY

## KICY Radio

Because we had decided at the beginning to sponsor a different group each year, it was always exciting to see how the Lord would bring a cause to our minds. It wasn't too many years before our market regulars would ask us, "Who do you plan to support next year?" For many years, I had been supporting KICY radio in Nome, Alaska.
I so admired the staff's dedication in providing support for the people of western Alaska, not to mention their fortitude in living in such a remote area.

Salmon, anyone?

Toward the end of the marketing season, we had the opportunity for them to sign up for a free salmon dinner to be cooked by Dennis Weidler, KICY station manager. He arranges salmon dinners four times a year sponsored by churches to present Station KICY and their outreach. We were working with a secular group and hosted 75–100 people. Praise God!

Virginnia and I had KICY hoodies to wear when the weather got cooler. We had started dressing alike earlier in the year when we had T-shirts with our logo and buttons made to call attention to our project. We also had brochures to tuck into a bag that gave information on our projects if customers wanted.

We have never received negative comments and people seem to be amazed that we donate all our proceeds and more to the projects. (MG)

## Give and It Will Be Given unto You

## Fruitful Mission

Bleak. That was the word that sprang to mind for twenty-six-year-old Virginnia Swenson when she arrived in Nome, Alaska. A young woman with a passion for travel, she had accompanied her uncle, Reuben Nelson, to that distant outpost to visit a new radio station pioneered by the Evangelical Covenant Church. Reuben was an early supporter of the mission, and Virginnia's family knew several of the people involved in developing the station. KICY would soon begin broadcasting daily to the isolated native population in the western part of the forty-ninth state, a place of few roads and long winters. The year was 1959.

Fast-forward fifty years. KICY continues to broadcast to western Alaska, and it is still very much a mission, supported by churches and individuals and staffed by full- and part-time volunteers.

Every day, its AM and FM stations deliver Christian music and programming to a widespread network of villages challenged by terrain and climate. KICY also broadcasts to parts of the Russian Far East, reaching that formerly closed country with the gospel. And Virginnia, now seventy-seven, is celebrating its anniversary—and the anniversary of her visit there—by making jam. Lots of jam.

Marianne Peters,
*The Covenant Companion*

---

"People were calling us the 'jam ladies,'" says Marjorie. "We came up with the name Vista Sisters, and things really blossomed after that." The sisters sell eight-ounce jars of jam in thirty-two flavors.

## About KICY Radio

*The Covenant Companion*

- KICY is owned by the Arctic Broadcasting Association, a 501(c)3 nonprofit, affiliated corporation of the Evangelical Covenant Church.
- KICY first signed on the air on Easter Sunday, April 17, 1960.
- The station broadcasts at 50,000 watts, twenty-four hours a day and is operated by full- and part-time volunteers and supported by donations.
- KICY serves more than forty villages in the area known as "bush Alaska." There are no roads. Available transportation includes four-wheelers, boats, snowmobiles, or airplanes. Most inhabitants are native Alaskans living a subsistence lifestyle much the way their ancestors did. Travel is sometimes impossible because of the harsh weather.
- KICY's Ptarmigan Telegraph allows listeners to send personal messages to one another over the air. This is especially helpful in the summer when people have gone to their fishing or prospecting camps, where the only device they may have is a battery-operated radio.
- The station's most popular program is CareForce. At 9:02 every weekday morning, listeners can hear a devotional from a local pastor who then reads and prays for the requests that have been phoned in by listeners.
- KICY has been broadcasting Christian programming to the Russian Far East since the station was established. Luda Kinok, a native Russian, works from 11 p.m. to 4 a.m., bringing current news, weather, and music to the broadcast, along with a Russian version of the program CareForce, led by Russian pastors.
- KICY is the only commercial radio station in the United States licensed by the FCC to broadcast into another country in their language.

For more information go to www.kicy.org

## Gustavus Alumni

Vista sisters' jam for missions
After Marjorie Swenson Gores '50 (left) and her sister Virginnia Swenson '54 returned to their childhood family farm near Vista, MN, they looked for ways to get reacquainted with people in the area. Not wanting to see area fruit go to waste, making jams and jellies seemed to be a natural project. They now produce 32 varieties, which they sell at farm markets. Since 2008 they have donated all proceeds to missions, including Bibles for the World, Mission Aviation Fellowship, and a Christian radio station in Nome, Alaska, that reaches a large area including Russia. Sales have doubled since they designated their profits to missions.

It seems that conventions and the busy springtime work go hand in hand. Because of the heavy snow this past winter, the ground was insulated, and in two weeks, our snow was gone. The ground absorbed the water, and the roads were free of frost ruts. What a miracle, as we usually have mud for weeks.

The cardinals are back, rototilling goes on, and we are preparing for the farmers market. This year we will give proceeds to KICY, a Christian radio station in Nome, Alaska. They are celebrating fifty years of serving remote areas by radio, even into Russia.

In 1959, I traveled with my uncle to see the beginnings of KICY. The town was just one street and a few homes. At that time, the missionary had a thousand-mile territory. Soon they started flying medicine, food, missionaries etc. to these areas. (The missionary was also a doctor at first.) Operations now are just on a larger scale and shift with the tundra. (Virginia Swenson, New Richland)

## The Smile Train
Changing the World One Smile at a Time

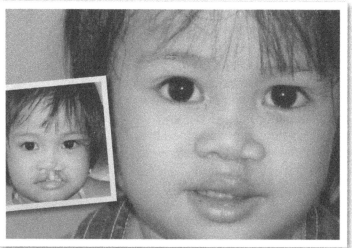

After the first three projects of BFW, MAF, and KICY, we chose our first non-Christian work, which was Smile Train. This group with its total emphasis on repairing cleft palates of children, almost total volunteer workers and staff brought much positive public response. We had a banner on the front of our table and handouts to publicize the work.

Along the line, we found a toy locomotive that inspired us to create "passenger cars" out of boxes coming behind the locomotive. Picture us, please, as we used tape, scissors, and cardboard! (This is Farmers Market?) For each $250 of sales, we added a smiley face to our cars, and soon, the public was checking on our progress week to week.

When the market season was complete for 2011, we were amazed and blessed to have provided for forty cleft surgeries. What an amazing God we have! (MG)

It took a long time to break out of winter. Now the break in could cause a break down, like with the rototiller.

This year, the proceeds from Vista Sisters' jams and jellies will go to the Smile Train. People seem to be excited about the project, so we hope to have another rewarding year.

When it is warm enough, it is great to sit outside sip coffee and watch God's display. (Virginia Swenson, New Richland RUAEA Newsletter)

Creating a "passenger car"

## Bridges for Peace

Both Marge and I have been to Israel several times and have known our Christian responsibility in helping support the nation. In 2012, we chose Bridges for Peace to be the recipient of our  market proceeds. However, we didn't get a response as soon as we needed, so we chose Bible League in Crete, Illinois. As soon as we were committed to Bible League, we heard from Bridges for Peace. It turned out our contact had been in Israel so our message was not received. (Perhaps we need e-mail after all.) Our solution was to work for both organizations, thinking we will be doubly blessed! The Lord's kind favor opened up a matching fund for one of our missions, and we truly thank the Lord. Our cause for Israel was to aid in food for the children and stockpile food for their survival in the times of conflict.

It is said that everything comes around and back to you. On our first trip to India, I had the opportunity to visit a synagogue in Sielmat where a small group of Jewish believers lived and worshiped. In a 2013 publication of *Bridges for Peace*, an article of immigration to Israel from northeast India appeared. The group was from the Bnei Menashe community in India. The ten tribes of Israel were never lost. (VS)

## Far Removed Yet Not Forgotten

Bridges for Peace, February 2013

Today, some of the descendants of Israelites from the northern kingdom are coming home to Israel. One such group is called the Bnei Menashe (Sons of Manassah). Michael Freund, the head of the Shavei Israel (Return to Israel) charity, has been the mover and shaker behind their recognition, immigration, and absorption. After much negotiation, they have been given permission to come to Israel. The cost to relocate this people group will be huge—millions!

Thanks to the help of many Christian friends like you, Bridges for Peace has been a significant partner in assisting the Bnei Menashe. This is in addition to assisting immigrants from many countries of the world. A few months ago, we told you about a group coming from Peru. They are now arriving in the city of Ramie.

The Bible predicted the day when both groups, Judah and Israel, would return!

"He will set up a banner for the nations, And will assemble the outcasts of Israel, And gather together the dispersed of Judah from the four corners of the earth." (Isa. 11:12)

"In those days the house of Judah shall walk with the house of Israel, and they shall come together out of the land of the north to the land that I have given as an inheritance to your fathers." (Jer. 3:18)

I became acquainted with Bible League about thirty years ago when the president was on a flight I was working. He was returning from China and Bible distribution in Asia. We had a very interesting conversation, and I started to support the league. Besides distributing Bibles, they also start local native home churches, supplying Bibles and teaching material around the world. It's been my joy to have helped start eighteen such church units with training and encouragement.

I was amazed by how so many customers were acquainted with Bible League. One lady ran a thrift store that gave a percentage to mission work overseas for Bible League. I hadn't been aware that they had this operation and several more around the country. (VS)

## CHANGING A COMMUNITY

Your church planter has completed our training, reporting these cumulative impacts as a result of your sponsorship:
- Evangelistic contacts ........................................................634
- People completing an evangelistic Bible study to receive God's Word ..............................................................64
- People completing a discipleship Bible study to receive God's Word ..............................................................114
- Bible study groups ..............................................................14
- Commitments to Christ ....................................................188
- New church members/baptism ..........................................0

Your church planter loves the Bible and has successfully moved people from decision to disciple. This is the impact God has orchestrated through your church planter sponsorship. Thank you for your heart to reach lost and seeking people today; you're making an impact for eternity!

How easy it is to form a good opinion of ourselves and be proud of our own accomplishments! Let us ask God to turn His searchlight on our souls that we might see ourselves as He sees us. We need the Holy Spirit to burn self out of our heart that we might be filled with the Spirit of Christ.

—PAW

Thank you so much for the delicious baked goods and the fascinating stories of adventure.

—Kimberlee

Loved talking to you. Vista Sisters! What amazing products! All the best to you!

—Betty Gordon, Duluth, MN

Thank you for ministry, wonderful outreach, great smiles, and loving attitude.

Your friend in Christ, Rudy N., Bloomington, MN

# Alaska
CHRISTIAN COLLEGE (ACC)

In 2013, our decision to support ACC in Soldotna, Alaska, was based on a timely visit in October 2012 when college president Dr. Keith Hamilton called us and arranged a breakfast meeting at an area restaurant. Keith had heard about us, and as we talked over coffee, we discovered he was proposing we consider supporting ACC with our Farmers Market proceeds in 2013. He just happened to have some T-shirts and pamphlets along! Here was a salesman who was a major fundraiser for ACC.

Formed in the year 2000, their express purpose is to reach native Alaskan youth living in remote villages. The school's mission is to use biblically based education and surroundings to build character and create a desire to serve as a follower of Christ. Many graduates go back to their native villages to start youth groups and Bible studies to try and improve the lives of the villagers. This year they have 51 students, and the enrollment continues to grow.

As we left the breakfast meeting and drove home, we laughed and said, "Well, that's settled."
Actually we were impressed and liked the no-nonsense attitude. *It was a great year!* (MG)

## Hi, ACC Partners!

Once again we welcome another class—13th year of educating and forming disciples of Jesus Christ! We are thrilled to initiate the two AA programs as described in this newsletter. What an enormous difference this will make for the future of Alaska Native young people!

I ask you today to send a generous special gift to help us get these two degrees off the ground this fall. Please consider today joining our mission of reaching Alaska with your gift. An Alaska-sized thanks,

*Keith J Hamilton*

# Charitable Concoctions

Marjorie Gores and Virginnia Swenson moved back to the New Richland area more than 30 years ago and began baking as a way to get reacquainted with the community. They soon decided to donate the profits to charities all around the world.

By Jennifer Holt
*Waseca County News*

**How and why they began selling baked goods for charity**

Two sisters from Otisco Township wanted to get involved in the community after returning from California—and they never expected it would turn into an annual endeavor to give back to charity.

Marjorie Gores and Virginnia Swenson began making jams and jellies years ago, selling them at local farmers markets. The Vista Sisters quickly gained notoriety for their jams and decided every year they would donate their profits to a different charity.

After living in California for more than 30 years, the sisters moved back and felt a little bit "out of it" and wanted to get reacquainted with the community.

When they moved back, they felt they lost a whole generation of people they knew before they moved out west—people moved out and new residents moved in.

"We've always given money to missions, which is nothing new," Gores said. "Our intent was to get acquainted with everyone and do something; if I wasn't doing this, I wouldn't be doing anything."

In 2003 the sisters took their first trip to India and after witnessing the famine and hardships of the area, they decided to give back to Bibles for the World, a program that distributes Bibles to developing nations.

"Once we said we were going to give proceeds back to Bibles for the World, our sales doubled," Swenson said, "and that was really exciting."

### What they give back to charity

Over the last 10 years they began making the jams. The sisters now have 32 varieties of jams and jellies they offer for sale during the summer at farmers' markets in Waseca County and in Bloomington. They begin cooking in January to get ready for their summer sales—and all the packaging is done themselves.

"People really like it," Swenson said. "They tell us we have such good varieties and are always asking for more."

They said their mother was talented, always making good use of the yard's produce. When they began cooking themselves, seven to 12 jars per batch was more than they could consume themselves, so they decided to start selling the rest.

Two days before each market, they'll start baking various goodies they sell in addition to the jams.

They also sometimes make handmade greeting cards and hand-stitched quilted pillows.

### How they have benefited from volunteering

"Personally, it's just made us so aware that we're guided in what we do," Swenson said. "It gives a purpose to living."

What started as something to get involved in has turned into something that keeps them busy in the community.

We feel like it's kind of an inspiration for the other elderly people," Gores said. "I know there are many other people who do great things, and this is ours. Our mission is to make as much money as we can to give to charity."

### What advice would they give to someone who is considering volunteering their time?

Swenson said people must be passionate and enthusiastic about what they want to volunteer for.

Gores said even despite her arthritis, she was able to find something she is able to do and enjoys doing.

# Work in Progress

# Jam and Jelly Flavors

Apple Butter
Apple
Apricot
Blackberry
Blueberry
Boysenberry
Cherry Tart
Cherry Sweet
Cherry Berry
Concord Grape
Crab Apple
Cranberry
Elderberry
Gooseberry
Hot Pepper
Mint
Mango
Orange Marmalade

Pear Butter
Peach
Piña Colada
Plum
Raspberry
Rhubarb
Black Raspberry
Strawberry Rhubarb
Strawberry
Tomato
Queen's Delight (blueberry/ raspberry)
Rhubarb Delight (rhubarb, pineapple, cherry)
Pumpkin
Lavender
Rosemary
Basil

Some of 42–45 varieties
Samplers: Assorted, All-Berry,
Rhubarb (in season), 4-Grape pkg.

# Jam and Jelly Making

Making Butters:

In batches, I puree the fruit with the sugar and spices (divided up). This gives a sure blend of ingredients. I also prefer to use a 3" deep pan, about 9 × 14 and place in 210-degree oven. Check and stir every 15 minutes, and sooner as it thickens. As you make butters, they have a tenancy to sputter, so watch your arms.

Making Jams:

Always use the best fruit in ripeness and color.

I use one cup less of fruit (most of the time) and add one cup water or one cup of juice. The fruit can be very concentrated, so this gives a less strong flavor. Also, I use 1/2–1 c. less sugar as I prefer the taste of the fruit over the taste of sugar. When cooking the jam or jelly, sample the sweetness about two minutes before it's done and adjust to your liking. This is also a good time to test for the setting up by putting several drops in a small bowl to see if it gels. There is time then to add a little more pectin or hot water as the situation requires.

I always follow the recipe given on the pectin box. It has the times for cooking and when to add the sugar, etc. My recipes given here are my basic ingredients.

A little lemon juice added gives a fresh taste. Just 1/4 tsp. of lemon juice is often an ample amount to add, unless recipe calls for more.

Because of the long winters and lack of fresh picked fruit, I often use fresh frozen that is packaged in bulk at most grocery stores. Check the color and dates.

The main advice is that you should have fun and don't be afraid. *Hot jars* and *lids are a must*! (VS)

# Minnesota Plums

After steaming the plums and the pulp cools, the pits are removed. I package the pulp two cups per freezer bag. When it's time to make the jam, two cups are ground up, and the bottled juice is added to give the correct measure for the jam.

Me and my sistr Loved the Plum Jam

Aprons courtesy of the Hmar

The sisters put in long days from February through October, selling their products at several area farmers markets and a nearby resort, doing all the preparing, marketing, selling, and delivering themselves. Sometimes they work twelve hours straight. "It's tiring," says Virginnia with a chuckle. "We're not as young as we used to be." "If we get really tired, we think about why we are doing it," says Marjorie. "Then we get a burst of energy and take off again!" —*The Covenant Companion*

Dozens of jars get washed.

# Rhubarb

Pink and Green

Because Virginnia and I believe in miracles, we are also looking for them to happen to us. We are thrilled at the many instances, although they may be small in nature. What others are apt to term luck, we usually consider a miracle (or God's leading).

When we were ready to package our seven rhubarb variations into a sampler, Virginnia asked me what colors we should use to wrap the jars. Our choices are usually governed by the fact that we always have a red Frisbee as the base! But this time, I was feeling spring fever apparently, as I answered, "How about pink and green? They're the colors of rhubarb."

What I'm picturing in my mind is a pastel color, not dark or vivid in hue. We stopped at our local Dollar Store and Virginnia went in to see what selections they had. The clerk was very discouraging to her request for cocktail napkins. "I'm all out of cocktail napkins. I don't even have white ones. All I've got are pink and green!"

They were perfect. Luck, you might say—but we felt the Lord was smiling down on us and showing us that He approved! (MG)

If it's spring, it's *rhubarb*!
   Taking the stalks early makes the most delicate jam and mild pies.
   When using early rhubarb, use half the sugar and add more as needed. I've actually used two cups less sugar, as it's sweet enough. I much prefer the taste of the fruit over too much sugar. (Virginnia Swenson)

# Crab Apples

Crab-apple pickles are a two-day affair. A person has to sort the bad apples out, then cook the others for a short time in brine, transfer to a crock, cover the apples with the hot brine, cover, and leave overnight.

In the morning, strain and recook the brine. Pack the cool apples in jars, cover with brine, leaving some room for expansion. Seal tightly and hot-bath the jars.

Crab-apple jelly is easy to make from the juice. It's a favorite!

# Minnesota Red Grapes

Much comes from one Concord grapevine!

**Concord Grape Jam**
3 c. juice
3 oz. pectin (whisk in)
1 c. ground grape pulp
1/2 c. lemon juice
3/4–1 c. water
7 1/4 c. sugar
(a little hot water as needed)
Yield: nine 8-oz.

# Oranges

Being from Minnesota with long winters, we love the cut-up orange and grapefruit for breakfast.
We cut the rind from the orange before sectioning the fruit. The rind is cut in strips for marmalade, or one can grind it for zest. The same can be done with the

*Love your labels! Can't wait to try the marmalade!*

Cutting rind slices

lemon. The rinds are put in plastic bags (two oranges at a time) and frozen. When it's time to make the marmalade, the strips are ready and the Florida OJ with pulp makes the process easier.

Orange Marmalade
Combine strips of 4 oranges and 2 lemons in kettle with 2 1/2 c. water, and 1/8 tsp. baking soda. Bring to boil, cover, and simmer 20 min. Whisk 3 oz. pectin into 3 c. Fla. OJ with pulp and 1/2 c. lemon juice. Pour in kettle and add 1 c. water. (There should be a total of 7 c. liquid). Have a rolling boil for 2 minutes, then add 9 to 9 1/2 c. sugar. Boil again 4 minutes. Skim if needed, then jar.

Blueberry Jam with OJ

In kettle, add 3 1/4 c. wild blueberry. Whisk 3 oz. pectin with 1 c. water, 1/4 c. lemon juice, and 1/2 c. OJ with pulp. Bring to rolling boil for 2 minutes. Add 6 c. sugar and boil 4 minutes (add 1–1 1/2 c. hot water to thin). Always test jam/jelly in final 4 minutes by placing several drops in a dish to test for setting up. It should not run.

Florida's Natural
PREMIUM
Squeezed From Our Fresh Oranges
NOT FROM CONCENTRATE

My favorite vendors at the Bloomington Farmers Market. Love those pies!

M R

It's hard to decide… which pie will it be?

# Elderberries

The elderberry is a natural berry in Minnesota. The white blossoms can be found in ditches and nearly anywhere that field sprays have not been used.

It looks much like a Queen Anne flower. When each tiny berry is ripe, it is black in color. They ripen unevenly, so cut out the green ones. It is important to not leave any stem, as it would give an unpleasant woody flavor to the jelly.

The harvest of the elderberry takes time, so pick a shady spot.

The sisters grow much of their own fruit—grapes, boysenberries, rhubarb, and apples—and they accept donated fruit as well. They are always on the lookout for sales of sugar, flour, and other ingredients. They attribute their work ethic to their heritage. "We were brought up to not let anything go to waste," says Marjorie, who says her mother was the one who first taught them how to make jam.

"We would love to have her with us," says Virginnia. "She would get a real kick out of this."
—*The Covenant Companion*

The Elderberry

Our steamer gets a workout!

# Peaches and Pears

Pears, as well as peaches, are so good canned. We always had pints/quarts canned for the winter to use as sauce or a salad with cottage cheese. When we are working, we quite often will have the cottage cheese, pear, and crackers as a picker-upper.

The juice is also good when used with sparkling water and Stevia as sweetener.

Pear butter and peach butter are very tasty and compete with the apple butter. We make our butters in the oven, for they are easier to control and will not scorch.

# Tomatoes

Don't let the box fool you. We raised these beauties.

Even when I lived in the San Francisco area, I had a small garden in the backyard. Country girl at heart!

Tomato Jam

2 1/4 c. tomato pulp
1/4 c. lemon juice and peel (ground)
3 oz. pectin (whisk in)
3 1/2 c. sugar
(a little hot water, as needed)
Yield: four 8 oz.

Rhubarb Jam

6 c. rhubarb, chopped
1 c. water
3 oz. pectin
6 c. sugar
1 Tbsp. lemon juice
6 c. sugar

Rhubarb Delight
(can be doubled)

6 c. rhubarb, chopped
4 c. sugar
1/2 jar maraschino cherries,
crushed with juice
1 10-oz. can crushed
pineapple
Mix and let sit overnight in
fridge to make juice. In the
morning, bring to full boil
10 minutes. Remove and add
2 Tbsp. butter and 2 small
pkgs strawberry Jell-O. Jar and
seal or put up frozen. Nine
8-oz.

Strawberry Jam

5 c. crushed strawberries
1 c. water
3 oz. pectin
6 c. sugar
1/2 tsp. lemon juice
3/4–1 c. hot water

Mango Jam

1 c. mashed mango
2 c. mango juice, whisk in 3
oz. pectin
1/4 c. lemon juice
5 c. sugar

Mango Butter

6 large mangoes, peeled and
cubed
1 c. lime juice (6 limes)
Puree in 2 batches until
smooth. Combine with 1 c.
sugar and 2 cinnamon sticks.
In 4-qt. pot, bring above to
simmer, reduce heat to low
and simmer 60–70 minutes.
Stir often till consistency of
apple butter.

# Packaging

Labeling jars on the side and the top

Even our bags get fancied up!

# Baking

Our Hoosier cabinet always
gets a workout.

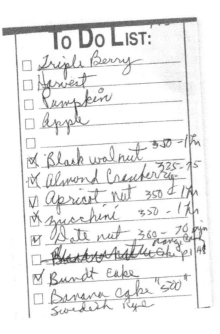

Baking was to supplement
the jams and jellies.
Somehow it got to be a big
part of our market produce.
We're not a bakery! Are we?
Hmm.
We work together, of course,
but Marge is the baker.
Virginnia makes the yeast
breads. ~ M.G.

It didn't take us more than a couple markets to realize that the demand in baked goods was for smaller sizes in cakes, pies, and breads. The little round individual pie tin met the desires of our customers, as did the smaller bread sizes. We also have used crumble toppings entirely, rather than a pastry topping.

There are many excellent pie crust recipes to explore. Here is the one I use which has proved to be consistent in flavor, flakiness, and firmness.

In food processor, mix 3 c. flour, 1 tsp. salt, and 1 1/4 c. shortening. Add 1 egg to 5 Tbsp. buttermilk and add to mixture.

Divide dough into 4 equal parts. May be stored in the fridge 2–3 days. Each part = one crust.

Some sample recipes below have proven to be very popular. They each call for a double crust, although (as I mentioned earlier) I always use the crumble-top crust for the small pies.

Apple-Cherry Pie usually has toasted almonds, 1/2 c. chopped sprinkled in bottom crust. Add 1/2 tsp. ground cardamom to the sugar-flour mixture. Use 1 c. tart red cherries to 5–6 c. apples.

Very Berry Pie uses more raspberries and blueberries and fewer strawberries, as I want a less-prominent strawberry taste. This gives me 5 c. fruit. The sugar-flour mixture has 1/4 tsp. nutmeg. Add 1 Tbsp. lemon juice and 1/2 tsp. almond extract to the fruit.

Peach-Raspberry Pies were always the first to go (after any kind of rhubarb). This pie was always very juicy, and I had to cut down on the amounts of fruit as well as increase the thickener somewhat. Here is what I use:

Place 2 c. raspberry on bottom crust, sprinkle 1/2 sugar-flour mixture over; add 2 c. sliced or chopped peaches over; cover with remaining sugar-flour mixture. Dot with butter and cover with top crust.

The pie is great if one adds 1/4 tsp. cinnamon to the sugar-flour mix and sprinkles fruit with 1 tsp. lemon juice and 1/4 tsp. almond extract.

Blueberries may be substituted for raspberries and then omit the almond extract.

Marge crushing the cardamom while taking a break from mowing

Checking the spices

# Pie Making

A good pastry is all-important to a delicious pie. Spend time in making your choice and then use good, fresh ingredients. Read your cookbook. My book has an area called a "pie crust clinic." It asks:

What makes pie crust...
> Tough? It has five reasons!
> Crumbly? Three reasons.
> Shrink and lose its shape? Three reasons.
> Fail to brown? Six reasons.
> Brown unevenly? Six reasons.
> Stick to the bottom of pan? Two reasons.
> Have an unpleasant flavor? Four reasons.

But be of good cheer! *Follow directions*, handle pie dough gently, don't pull on it, don't overmix or reroll too much. Use common sense and fresh ingredients; above all, compliment the cook when you have enjoyed a good slice of pie!

Apple pie is all-American, you know. Sometimes I don't use any spice if the apple is especially tasty.

Explore using different combinations of fruit. Instead of a plain apple pie, for example, see my recipe for apple-cherry.

Sprinkle very finely chopped nuts into your pastry as you mix it together. Sprinkle finely chopped nuts on the bottom crust before adding fruit. Substitute brown sugar for some of the white for added flavor. Blueberry flavor is greatly enhanced by adding 1/4 c. orange juice plus a touch of cinnamon (1/2–1 tsp.)

Triple Berry is always popular, but if using strawberry, use only 1 cup instead of 2, as its flavor might dominate the other berries. Thickening ingredients may be substituted for each other, such as flour, cornstarch, or quick-cooking tapioca.

General Hints

1.  Best taste comes from using the best ingredients, such as freshly squeezed lemon juice, fresh zest (lemon or orange).
2.  If possible, grate your own nutmeg. You'll be shocked at the difference.
3.  Whenever butter can be used, do it for the flavor.
4.  Pure vanilla makes all the difference.
5.  Quick breads should *only* be mixed until moistened.
6.  Parchment paper cleanup is much easier.
7.  Wire racks for cooling baked goods are a big asset.
8.  Cookie dough measured out by a scoop makes for same-size cookies.
9.  Be sure pie thickeners are well mixed with fruit to avoid a doughy filling.
10. Fruit pies *require a hot oven* to prevent sogginess.

A basic fruit pie recipe looks like the following:

Pastry for a two-crust pie:
3/4–1 c. sugar
2 Tbsp. flour
1/2–1 tsp. cinnamon
1/8 tsp. nutmeg
1/4 tsp. salt
5–6 c. fruit
2 Tbsp. butter

Mix first five ingredients together and add to fruit. Place all in pie pan and dot with butter. Adjust top crust and flute edges. Cut vents in top crust. Bake in hot oven until crust is browned and fruit juices are bubbling. - M.G.

Another two sisters who form part of our backup group
Thank you, Insty-Prints!

A sense of purpose and connection
increases longevity.

*Dear ladies,*

*Was so nice to see you at crossings. I can't wait for my friends to open their gift of jellies. Of course, the other one I kept for myself.*

*Keep doing what you're doing because it is just wonderful.*

*Your customer and friend,*
*Sandy*

# Our Motivation

## Our Motivation

Why Me?   For we are His workmanship,
created in Christ Jesus for good
works, which God prepared
*beforehand* that we should walk in
them. (Ephesians 2:10)

But How?   And my God shall supply all
your need according to His
riches in glory by Christ Jesus.
(Philippians 4:19)

Our Goal   Each one's work will become clear;
for the Day will declare it… if
anyone's work which he has built on
it endures, he will receive a reward.
(1 Corinthians 3:13a, 14)

Our Motive   But without faith it is impossible
to please Him, for he who comes
to God must believe that He is,
who diligently seek Him. (Hebrews
11:6)

# Acknowledgments

Bibles for the World
Box 49759
Colorado Springs, CO
80949-9759

Mission Aviation Fellowship
(MAF)
Box 47
Nampa, ID 83653-0047

KICY
Box 820
Nome, AK 99762-9985

Smile Train
Box 96246
Washington, DC 20090-6246

Bridges for Peace
Box 410037
Melbourne, FL 32941-0037

Bible League, Int.
1 Bible League Plaza
Crete, IL 60417

Alaska Christian College
35109 Royal Place
Soldotna, AK 99669

Credits:
Insty-Prints, Owatonna, MN
Bibles for the World
*Covenant Companion*
(Dec. 2010)
*G.A. College Quarterly* (2011)
*Waseca County News* (2013)
RUAEA (UAL retired news)

# Suggested Reading

Good Reading!

*Beyond the Next Mountain*
by Dr. R. Pudaite, book and/or CD

*Ptarmigan Telegraph*
The beginning of radio station KICY, by Greg
Asimakoupoulos

*End of the Spear*
Five men martyred in jungles of Peru, by Steve Saint
The movie tells the story from the perspective of Steve
Saint and Mincayani, one of the tribesmen who killed the
missionaries—five members of MAP.

*The Million-Dollar Living Room*
by Krause

The Holy Bible

I pray that your partnership with us in the faith may be effective in deepening your understanding of every good thing we share for the sake of Christ. (Philemon 1:6, NIV)

There goes the
# Jam Van!

CPSIA information can be obtained
at www.ICGtesting.com
Printed in the USA
FFHW021823271119
56124856-62237FF

9 781644 924358